DEATH OF YAZDGERD

A play

by

Bahram Beyzaie

Translated by

Manuchehr Anvar

Bisheh Publishing – San Francisco, USA

Death of Yazdgerd

A Play by Bahram Beyzaie

Translated by Manuchehr Anvar

Written in : 1979
Translated in : 1995
Cover Design : Mohsen Valihi

Copyright 2022 by Bahram Beyzaie
All rights reserved, including the right to reproduce this book
or portion thereof in any form whatsoever.

Library of Congress Control Number: 2022933241
ISBN: 978-1-7355686-6-9

The publication of this book was made possible by the Hamid
and Christina Moghadam Program in Iranian Studies at
Stanford University.

Bisheh Publishing – San Francisco, USA
Bisheh.publishing@gmail.com
www.bisheh-publishing.com
Published in the United States of America

DEATH OF YAZDGERD

• Yazdgerd III, of the Sasanian Dynasty, was the last of Iranian kings before the Islamic era. During his reign, Arab invasion of Iran intensified and with his death in AD 651, a lengthy epoch in Iranian history came to an end.

•• Ancient Iranian calendar was a fragmented one. A new calendar started at the first year of the throning of a new king and ended with his death. The time period between the end of one era and the beginning of another, known as Shâmiran, was indeed a period of chaos, disorientation and timelessness. The play "Death of Yazdgerd" is about a Shâmiran. It depicts a Day Zero of the Year Zero of the Iranian calendar - a time when an old order has collapsed and a new order has yet to emerge.

••• For ancient Iranians the King was a symbol of glory and divine destiny. And if a King's glory was lost due to his misdeeds, his reign was doomed to collapse. In such event, it was a common belief that only the King's death could spare the country from further disaster.

"...Thereupon Yazdgerd fled towards Marv and sought refuge in a watermill. The miller, longing for His treasures, killed Him in sleep... [AD 651]."

History!

Characters

Woman

Miller

Girl

Commander

Mubad (Zoroastrian Priest)

Captain

Soldier

[Inside a watermill, half-lit. A corpse is on the floor, a golden mask on its face. Mubad chanting above the corpse's head, praying and burning incense. The miller, standing still with a terrified expression. Woman, like a ghost, gets up; and girl shrieks.]

Miller   No, reverend masters
lofty Commanders
clad in armour from top to toe!
That which you administer now
is not justice
but rank tyranny.
This indeed is the place
where his blood was shed
- this uninvited guest -
but I'm not to blame for it.
He had already opted for death.
No, my armour-clad masters
what you do to us
is not what we deserve.

[Captain claps. Soldier kneels]

Commander This is our verdict:
man, miller
with hands dipped in blood
up to the elbow!
You shall be put to death
presently
but not so easily.
You shall swing on the gallows
but not before your bones are crushed

and your joints pulled apart.
Your espouse shall be thrown into the oven
and your daughter's hide shall be stuffed
with straw.
The record of this horrible crime
will hang from city gates
and the name of the miller
shall be defiled forever.

Mubad May turbid darkness be cast away
from the dungeon of the flesh!
May light be liberated from darkness
and fire freed from smoke!
May turbid darkness be cast away
from the dungeon of the flesh...

Soldier Where can we get some wood?
Is there enough rope around here?

Woman Shameless blackguards that you are!
Will you kill us, or plunder us?

Captain Pull out the tent poles
and quickly raise the gallows.
As for the rope...

Woman Yes, make haste
lest we get away
and our tongue shall reveal
the disgraceful story of his flight
and make people laugh

	at the valiant Shâh! Yes, be quick!
Soldier	Give me leave to work my sword here and now. It'll get the job quickly done with only two thrusts and one cut.
Commander	Really? Only two thrusts and one cut? Is there another way?
Soldier	Takes a long time to make the gallows, Commander. Let me hang'em right here. Why bother about the gallows?
Commander	Simple-hearted man whereto are you galloping so fast? We're all commanders and captains of noble lineage and not looters and murderers. And this is administering Justice not an ambush! We do not kill them for the sake of killing. Their death is a retribution for shedding the blood of a gallant King the Commander of commanders possessor of all possessors King of all Kings

Shâh Yazdgerd
the son of Shâh Yazdgerd
who himself was one of the sons of
Yazdgerd the First.
This red rivulet you see here running
flows from him
who had royal blood
in all his four hundred and sixty six veins
and was placed above all men
by the hand of Ahurâ Mazdâ.
And now that the enemy is pressing
our throat
what better assistance could it be given
than the severing of the head from the
body.
And everybody knows that people
are the body
and the King is the head!

Girl   *[Moaning and writhing]*
          The King is not slain
          the King is not slain!

Captain   Is this not his body?

Miller   Do not make them laugh at us!

Girl   He is asleep
          dreaming about us.

Commander He was about to gather a great army

             and deliver the kingdom
             plain after plain
             from the countless hordes of the enemy.

Captain   What shattered hope!

Mubad   By the end of the millennium
             the cycle of the ewe shall come to an end
             and that of the wolf shall commence
             - demons trampling on angels.

Woman   No, no
             we did not kill him.
             You charge us with your own fancy.

Commander What a shameless lie!
             Where is he who found him slain
             by their hands?

             [To Captain]
             Did you not see these vultures
             clawing the carcass of the King?

Captain   Indeed, I was the first
             to set foot in this desolate ruin;
             and my hair stood on end
             - seeing what I saw.
             The idle millstone
             seemed as if it had never turned
             and these three
             - the miller, his wife and his daughter -

sat around the bleeding body of the King
moaning.
The King still in regal garb
more magnificent than ever.
Dust rising in an oblique shaft of light
rushing down from the casement
to shroud his lifeless frame.
The streak of the warm blood
snaking across the floor
and disappearing under the millstone.
Dark tokens of death scattered
everywhere.
All this shall haunt me to my dying day.
I'm still amazed at the flood of tears
these ruffians poured over their own victim.

Miller We wept not for him
but for ourselves.

Woman *[Cries]*
For my child!

Girl *[Weeping]*
My brother!

Woman I raised him on my heart's blood
till he was a comely youth.
My son
my only son
was taken to the battle
by your soldiers.

             And before the rising of the new moon
             they wanted me to reward them
             for bringing back his body
             soaked in blood
             and mangled with eight arrows.

Mubad   Men are all soldiers of death.
             Be brief woman
             and say if your sapling
             was of the same worth
             as our sovereign!

Woman   May my tongue wither
             if I say so!
             No, by heavens, no!
             For me
             he was of much greater worth!

Commander Huh!
             Did you hear that?
             It is thus that this kingdom
             is now falling to pieces.
             Say then you miller with a dead son
             have you revenged yourself upon the
             King?

Miller   Ay
             my breast was full of revenge
             but I did not kill him;
             not out of goodness,
             but fear.

Woman   "A King has followers who'd look for him," you said.

Miller   And you said that I was right.

Woman   And you said that you should not raise your hand against him.

Miller   And I did not raise my hand against him!

Girl   [Beside the corpse]
Our only witness sleeps here.

Mubad   I can no longer bear lies.
In the foulest of times
when the millennium comes to an end
men such as you
would be more than many.
And out of five words
four would be lies.
You have turned your mill
with our king's blood;
and a king is the shadow of Ahurâ Mazdâ.
So your cup will be filled with your own blood!
And desert dogs shall feast on your bones!
This is irrevocable;
and we have sworn that your household shall perish.

Miller   And the wind is already on its way.

And now
in the midst of storm
they spin the rope that'll presently press
my neck.
And mouthing curses
they raise the gallows for me.
Their thirsty swords
shall be satisfied only with my blood.
Out of their anger
they have raised a shield before me
throwing my words back at me
like broken javelins.
Ah, but where's the remedy?
O masters, draped in anger
know that I'm punished for my misery
and no other sin.

Mubad You're punished for your greed.
The demon that raised its head in you
was called avarice.
Tell us if you gazed at the King's
shining breast plate
or his knee-band
or belly-band
or leg-band?
We know well that the subordinate
long to rise above their superiors.
The runner behind
wants nothing better
than to overtake the one running ahead
of him.

	Or the loser what does he want but winning? The walker hates the rider and the beggar thirsts for the king's blood.
Miller	Even so I did not kill him - not out of detachment but fear.
Woman	"There are riders escorting the King who shall ride after him," you said.
Miller	Ignorant that I am I was afraid.
Woman	You then said that you should not raise your hand against him.
Miller	I did not raise my hand against him.
Girl	Our only witness sleeps here.
Soldier	*[Pole in hand, enters and exits]* A few pieces of wet wood were found in the cellar. This one can well stand the weight of the man.
Girl	*[Throws herself in her mother's arms]* Father's death

shall make me lonelier than ever.

Woman *[Separates herself]*
Lonely, dear daughter?
Fear not
for you too shall die quickly
and I with you.
Now enemies ride forth from every side
just as the eight winds blow
from the mountains and the slopes
from the forests and the plains
from the sea and the rivers
and from the wastelands and the deserts.
In the midst of this storm
standing
am I.
Look for the King's slayer not here
but out there.
The King was slain already by the King.
He who came here was a feeble little man.

Commander Speak, but not over much!

Woman Silent I cannot be.
If I do not say now what I have to say
then when can I say it?
Under the earth?
The King was not slain here.
He was dead before he came.

Commander *[To miller]*

Make her hold her tongue!

[To woman]
And you
do not call us oppressors!
Did not a man
lost in the storm
come to your battered mill?

Woman He did
like a shadow.
He was looking for death.

Commander Babble no more!
Speak man
before I whip you.
Did not a great man
arrayed as a king
come to this place?

Miller Would that I had gouged my eyes
with my own hands
when
standing at the threshold
I saw him descend the hill.

Commander Then he did come to this
forsaken ruin!

Miller Ay.

Commander On his own feet?

Miller Ay, he came.
He did.
And he was agitated.
He came in rags.

Commander This "he" you talk about
was the King of kings.

Miller How could we know?
He came here as a beggar.
To a place so dark and dank.
This forsaken pit.
He came like a frightened wayfarer;
so frightened that we took him for a
bandit
who
having looted people on the road
was now blowing out the lamp
with a terrified puff.

Woman He threw himself down in a corner
and asked for the casements to be closed.

Miller *[To girl]*
Was it not that your heart was jolted?

Woman He was surely a thief.

Miller Or a beggar.

How could we know?

Girl [Moaning]
Give me something to eat!

Commander Say now, man!
Before they raise your gibbet
tell us what the King told you.
Did he not think of going back to war
against the Tazians*?

Girl [Gets up]
"Give me something to eat" he said.

Miller Something to eat?
Here's the bread bundle.

Girl Dry bread?

Miller Should we bake you a loaf?

Girl Meat!
I'm hungry.
Give me a piece of meat!

Woman [Mockingly]
Meat!
Did you hear that?

---

* An archaic Persian term for fleet Arab attacking horseman.

Girl You sound as if you've never tasted meat;
or seen a partridge or a pheasant.
Ah, what am I saying?
Is there no sheep here
or goat
that I could buy for a piece of gold?

Miller It would've been good to have a goat
for our girl here is sick
and goat's milk is said to be her cure.

Girl I'm hungry
and you talk about the medication for
the girl!
Ah, what a mean hovel have I fallen into!
Where is this
and what wretches are you?
I didn't know that creatures outside
Ctesiphon
neither believed in God
nor followed the Magi.

Miller Ctesiphon!
Did you hear, woman?
All the flour that I make
goes to Ctesiphon.

Girl I'm hungry!

Woman Why didn't you stay in Ctesiphon
and eat as much as you wanted?

Girl   How could I eat this dry bread?

Woman   Dip it in water.
For guests
there's whey to go with it.

Girl   *[Weeping]*
He ate what was my dinner.

[Suddenly roars]
Shut your mouth you impudent whore!
Give me water!

Woman   *[Disgusted]*
We're ordered around
in our own house!

Miller   I don't think he's a beggar.
Beggars beg
but he takes.
He behaves like the master of the house.

Woman   His power
doubtless
comes from the gold he carries.
We must look into his bag, miller.

Miller   Be quiet and let him sleep!
Outside, there's storm everywhere.

[Girl covers the corpse with a piece of cloth]

Commander And while he slept
you looked into his bag.

Woman When we found all those royal pearls in
his bag
we took it that he was a bandit
who had robbed the King.

Mubad All those royal pearls
should have indicated to you
that he was a mighty king
the head of all heads
and the King of all kings.

Miller Do kings seek safety in flight?
Beg like beggars?
Steal their own belongings?
Disguise?
Noticing the regal garb
and the golden crown
he had concealed in the bag
we took him for a common thief
who had stripped a nobleman
of his clothes
and stolen his jewels.
Yes
all that we thought.

Girl [*Laughs*]
What a banquet
what a banquet it was!

And I was an invited guest.

[*Weeps*]
The King is not slain.

[*Cries out*]
Neighbours have abandoned us.
Foreign hordes are everywhere.
Take to your heels!

Miller No!
How could one really know
that he was the King?

Commander Curse on miseries
as well as glories of this world!
We followed him on swift horses
but he was far ahead of us
on his swifter mount.
And in the storm
we lost his track.
Darkness
- curse upon its demons -
holding the reins of our horses
took them where it willed.

Mubad Curse upon the evil Ahriman!

                    Twice
                    thrice
                    thirty times
                    a thousand times!

Commander Today
                    in the dimness of dawn
                    when heavens
                    like a crow's plumage
                    were a mix of darkness and light
                    our easy-paced horses boggled thrice.
                    We then let them lead us to this hovel
                    and
                    as we opened the door
                    the slashed body of the mighty King
                    spattered blood over the skies.

Captain   *[Snorting, draws]*
                    In this den of darkness
                    his blood shines
                    like a midnight sun.

Mubad   His wounds cry out for justice.

Captain   *[Attacking]*
                    They must be brought to death!

Commander *[Stops him]*
                    Yield no ground to anger!
                    Would you kill them now
                    with a thrust of your sword?

	Such a death would be a delight to them and very quick too. No! I'll tell you what they deserve: a slow death long and ugly a death that is ten times dying.
Captain	Pray Mubad, pray!
Mubad	How does the moon wax? How does the moon wane? Who causes it to rise and set except you o Ahurâ Mazdâ? May He come to our aid! May He come to comfort us! May He come to forgive us! May He come to give us victory!
Miller	Will there be prayers for us too when we are gone?
Mubad	I wish the impious dead! I wish the malevolent dead! I wish the devil-worshipper dead! May we never follow them! May we never succumb to them! May we never become their play things!

Captain May the world be cleansed of their names!
Is there no prayer to break the sleep of
death?

Mubad Better not speak of the impossible!
Tell us you noble soldier
how can it be broken
this sleep of death?

Captain *[Sadly]*
True
it cannot.

Miller His sleep was broken.
Don't you remember?
His sleep was broken.

Commander And you did not even recognize him
you blind-hearted ruffians!

Woman *[Suddenly]*
Hands off the bag!

Girl Look
he's rolling over.

Miller His sleep was broken.
Roaring, he woke up
sticking a hand under his head.

Woman One hand under the head

	searching for the satchel of gold and the other reaching for the sword.
Girl	Little man what're you looking for in the satchel?
Miller	Once he realized we knew about the pieces of gold he lost his bearing. "I'm the King," he cried "look at me, I'm the King." *[To Woman]* You laughed.
Girl	She did.
Miller	"I'm the King!"
Woman	Every man is king in his own house. And thus the king of this hovel is that miserable miller.
Miller	He drew his sword.
Girl	He drew his sword!
Woman	O King!

	If you're a warrior go fight the enemy! Why do you make war with us?
Miller	My head!
Girl	He held his head.
Miller	In my head there is a noise. The beating of a thousand drums. Soldiers as numerous as the sands of the desert.
Woman	This is a game to cheat us.
Girl	I think so too. Does he at all behave like a king?
Mubad	*[Kicks the ground]* It is him. It is he himself. I know that garb. That breast-plate, all in gold. Those greaves and elbow-pieces. That wrist-band and belly-band. All pieces of pure gold. Ay. I know the King.
Miller	"If you," said I

"with your helmet
armour
horse and shield
would run away
how could I
with my bare body and empty hands
stand still?"

Woman   He was frightened.
Couldn't stay within himself.
He was worn out.
He moaned and groaned
hitting his head
against this shade-pole.
He shouted that the enemy was coming.
He tried to hide the sword
the crown
and the regal garment.
He was looking for a place to hide.

Miller   I shouted.

Woman   He shouted.

Miller   I insulted him.

Woman   You did not.

Miller   I said
"O King!
Commander!

May your legs
that have carried you here
be broken!
Who will answer for my years of
suffering?
I've paid you tribute
every day of my life.
I've fed your horsemen.
And now that the enemy comes
you run away
and leave me hand-tied
you who tied my hands for many years!
And I no longer possess the knowledge
of war and the stomach for battle."
Yes!
I insulted him.
I hit him.

Woman You hit him.

Miller Once
twice
thrice.

Commander No fouler deed was ever done
anywhere
in this tormented land.
Why, and your hand didn't break?
You hit the King
and heaven and earth
stayed intact in their place?

Miller   I hit him.

Woman   You hit him
playfully and merrily
as they hit a clay-king in new year.
We never believed him to be the King.
Indeed he seemed nothing more
than a taunting liar.

Mubad   Silence!
Do you not know that the soul
stays hovering
over the body
for three days?
He is here
amongst us.
May he not suffer much
and give way to anger!
May he not speak!

Miller   The soul of the King
is here still.

Woman   Grab hold of him!
Close the casements
and do not let him escape!

Miller   Hit him!
Devastate him!
Crush him!

Commander What're you doing?

Miller Go to hell, soul
or speak
and say that we have told the truth!

Woman Speak, soul!
To what corner have you crawled?

[She hits]

Miller Where are you?
Here?
Take this!

[He hits]

Woman These torturers...
You've made them come here
and you yourself
aught to appease them.

Mubad Cease!
You act as if you're conjurers
and fiendish fellows.
Have you renounced your faith?

Woman If the soul of the King is here
let it then hear my curse:
be damned, o soul!

Mubad   *[Blows around into the air]*
Away with the magician's magic!
Away with the curser's curse!
Away with the evil-doer's evil!
To the four corners of the earth
did I banish them
and tied their thousand hands
with that invocation.

Woman   Block your ears
and do not hear
for I am looking for the foulest
language.

Commander Enough, woman!
I'll no longer suffer
the spirit of the King
so defiled.

Captain   Do you hear, woman?
These masters won't stand
your taunts and insults.

Woman   Are taunts and insults
also the property of the nobles
to be expended at their convenience?
No, they're stones and pebbles on the
ground
and I, too,
can throw a few of them at you.

Commander	You've added the red-hot rod to your punishment.
Woman	You can surely do worse than that!
Captain	Your tongue will be cut, woman!
Girl	*[Weeping]* Do not return their rage!
Woman	*[Roaring]* Why? *[Quiet]* My tongue knows much about your King. Did I not tell you he'd had a dream?
Mubad	A dream?
Woman	That which people see with their eyes closed.
Mubad	Now, that is strange! Do you hear? Our King must have had a ruffled dream. And as you ought to know there's always a secret in a dream. Tell me the secret, woman!

[Soldier enters]

Soldier Glad tidings, greatest Commander!
May the lamp of your fortune glow!
Your huntsmen have trapped a happy game:
a half-dead Tazian warrior
with bleeding wounds.

Captain A Tazian?

Soldier Their swords're curved
like the crescent moon.
And their robes are made of black wool.
And here is a louse!

Captain Loosen his tongue!
What does he know?

Commander What we need to know
is surely what he hides.

Captain What sort of a man is he?
A soldier?
A drummer?
A mule-driver?

Soldier He's a man, lost.

Captain He who is lost
is also a man.

	And how is he?
Soldier	Obstinate but hungry. Also much agitated.
Mubad	More agitated than the dream of a king?
Commander	Give him bread and whey
and then whip him
until he talks!
And ask him how many Tazians there are
and *where* they are.
What's on their minds?
Are they on horseback,
or on foot?
Going away
or getting nearer?
Passing or staying?
Why has he stayed behind?
Is he a messenger
an informer
or a scout?
Ask him why they destroy
burn
and wear black?
And this God they talk about
why is he so enraged?
Soldier	He doesn't answer, Commander.
Commander	Out of insolence?

Soldier He speaks no Persian.

Commander Tie him with a cord!
Hold him
and beat him with a stick
and make him talk!
Is the gallows ready?

Soldier What's not ready
is the furnace
to heat the rod.

Girl *[Covering her eyes]*
Hah!

Commander *[To miller]*
Do not hope in vain!

[To Soldier]
If you find no fire
poke his eyes with a cold rod.
Go, quick
and make him talk!

[Exit Soldier]

[To woman]
Now, what was that dream?

Mubad I'm listening to you too, woman.
You said that our King had had a dream.

Woman Yes
of the kind that only kings have.

Mubad Everyone knows that there are messages in
dreams.
Say, woman,
was there a secret in the king's dream?
Why was he agitated
when he woke up?

Woman He was afraid of you!

Commander Afraid... of us?

Woman People *like* you.

Commander Her tongue shall rid her of her head.

Woman Let it
if it cannot set me free!

Miller *[Pleading]*
What benefit such talk brings?

Woman And what loss?

Commander Tell us the dream!
Woman No, I close my lips.

Mubad Speak, woman,

	for thus orders the great Commander!
Woman	He ordered my tongue to be cut. How can a severed tongue speak?
Captain	That was out of anger. Speak, woman! The great Mubad is asking you. Should you be begged of?
Woman	What else could you do?
Girl	You frighten me!
Miller	Do not make worse what's already bad!
Woman	Don't come near me!
Captain	A warrior horseman such as I with grey hair is asking you.
Woman	I'm thirsty.
Mubad	Water!
Woman	Throw it away! *[To girl]* Light a fire! How dark it is!

	I see nothing. Is there no lamp here?
Mubad	What happened to her?
Commander	She wasn't so disturbed.
Girl	Why does he run away?
Miller	What are you hiding from?
Woman	*[Shouts]* A lamp!
Girl	What's happened?
Woman	I had a bad dream. Where are my interpreters?
Mubad	I'm here, your Majesty!
Woman	I dreamed I was riding my nimble horse in a boundless desert. Out of the earth grew not thorn or grass but groves of sharp swords.
Miller	My life was all an agitated dream. In such a ruin of a mill

which I've inherited from my
forefathers
what else can you have
but agitated dreams?

Woman Riding the wind
misfortune was coming.

Mubad In such an hour of the day
when there's neither light nor dark
and time moves neither forwards
nor backwards
such a dream
doubtless holds a message.

Woman A peerless horseman
sharp-speared
the warlike deity
the supportive Bahrâm
he who heartened me
the courageous one
who made the enemies tremble with fear
riding a bay horse
showed me the way
with the sweep of his banner.
Then a black wind broke out
a devilish rising wind
wild
unbridled.
And dust filling my eyes!
As I rubbed and opened them

           the sharp-speared and warlike deity
           the supportive Bahrâm
           even *he*
           had disappeared in the dust.
           Yes, I lost him in the tempest.

Captain Now we should know
           why the King was so frightened.

Miller We do not sell our guests to anyone.

Woman   Do you not?
           Why not?
           It is the best of deals.
           There are scores of buyers for my head.
           Many Commanders
           with words of fidelity on their lips
           secretly crave
           the throne of Yazdgerd.
           Are you not tempted by this gold?

Miller No!

Woman   You fool
           Make your bundle!
           You have here
           a marketable merchandise.
           Just take it to the buyers:
           my head in the sack.
           I shall write you the names of those
           who'd give you gold for it!

Girl	He's mad!

Woman	Mad? Hah!
Ay, mad!
My army was no more than a band of betrayers
who turned their back to me
and took to their heels
when
counting on them
I attacked the heart of the enemy.
My hair was not grey
until loneliness
pressed me tight
in its grip.
My terror was so great
that the nimble warriors were stunned
into opening a way for me.

Miller	Do you hear?
He's running away from friends
not enemies.

Woman	Good Thoughts
Good Words
and Good Deeds;
what's become of them?
The Oath of Courage;
what's happened to it?
And The Banner of The Blacksmith;
where has it gone?

| | Rocks are being thrown at me
from every side. |
|--------|------|
| **Girl** | These words truly show
that he's the King. |
| **Woman** | A king who has terror as his banner
and whose army is
but loneliness. |
| **Miller** | You didn't do well
making yourself known to me!
There's a pain in my heart.
You know
I had a son. |
| **Woman** | *[Weeping]*
No, don't speak! |
| **Miller** | In your name
they took him away
as a soldier.
And he returned
as if from the land of the dead. |
| **Woman** | *[Cries out]*
My green boy! |
| **Miller** | Now the injured spirit of the boy
rises in my head
and prompts me to kill you, King. |

Woman   That is well.
                  Let me cause it more injury
                  if this is truly so.

                  [Weeping]
                  Say what you will
                  but don't be harsh
                  with the sad spirit of my little boy
                  who's now descending
                  through the slanting lights of the roof
                  with a cracked skull
                  and a bronze face.

Girl   I'm truly frightened
                  piling terror upon terror.
                  Where is he?

                  [Shrieks]

                  My little brother
                  he's here!
                  He's pointing his finger at you.

Woman   *[To miller]*
                  Is it not time, now
                  to strike?

Girl   He's throwing up blood
                  and truly
                  there are drops of it on the floor.
                  My little brother!

[She grabs her mother's feet]

He ran away from the casement.
There's no blood there.
The roof light
is quite pale now.

Miller *[Feebly brings down the stick]*
No!
Every king is followed by horsemen
who will arrive
sooner or later.

Woman My boy, my boy!

Miller It seems from the howling of the wind
that my mill is swallowed
by the storm.

Commander The low-bred are very much like their
own lowness.
They're obsessed by their petty interests
and think only about bread and water
to satisfy their growling bellies.
Here
the King found nothing
but foulness
and callous hatred.
Look at these evil, obstinate animals
Who will not gain in humanity
even as the mighty

	bring them comfort and kings honor them with pity.
Woman	Coarse-tongued man! What comfort? Which pity? Look at those made-up faces! The high-born such as you have crushed our bones. You and all those freshly-draped upstarts you've plunged your snouts in our flesh. The difference between you and I is that sword dangling on your side.
Commander	Cut be your tongue!
Woman	That's why you wear a sword.
Girl	*[Dreamily]* Had a sack of flour been left I would've poured it on my head and turned white from top to toe. Thus perhaps dazzling Nâhid* would've taken me for an angel or washed *me* instead of her daughter

---

* Ancient Persian Goddess, protector of households and fertility

in some spring.

Woman What am I to say, men?
My husband is a distracted miller
who has ground nothing in this mill
but his own wretchedness.
A man regretting manhood
earning nothing
but sighs and sweat
in the coldest cold
and the hottest heat.
Such is my husband
the man to whom you promised your
sword.
What do we have
but a crumbling roof
and a groaning millstone
that goes round and round in circles?
He groaned even as this stone
and went round in circles
when the man in tatters
revealed his rank.

Miller *[Gets up]*
Why do you laugh?

Girl You're terrified.
I'd never seen a man so terrified.
You move left and right
and beat your knees.
You sigh

                    like a bird of sorrow
                    and all the while
                    steal yourself
                    even from yourself.
                    You're sad.

Miller   Silence!
                    Don't you hear a hubbub?
                    They say that ancient marble figures
                    standing in the Palace of A Hundred
                    Columns
                    have thrown down the gifts
                    they bore for a thousand years
                    and run away to the desert.
                    Did you ask something?

Girl   I laughed at you.

Miller   Ah, yes.
                    I also laughed much once.

Commander   Put on this gilded crown
                    and repeat the very words of the King.

Woman   [Putting clothes on the miller]
                    He was preoccupied.
                    He kept beating his wrinkled brow
                    with the palm of his hand.
                    He was preoccupied.

Miller   Not far from here

                    my horse threw me down
                    and vanished into the darkness of the storm.
                    The dead now come out of their crypts.
                    People are struck by lightning.
                    They go to meet the enemy
                    I've heard
                    with gifts of bread and dates.

Commander   Look!
                    He's speaking the words of the King.

Miller   What would the great think of a King
                    who's a fugitive in his own realm?

Woman   Nothing great.

Miller   A fugitive in my own realm
                    I move from house to house.
                    Everywhere a stranger
                    and not invited to any table.
                    My easy-paced horse
                    instead of carrying me to battle
                    took me away from it.
                    Shame on me!

Woman   What foolish prattle is this?
                    Don't try your game on us, you imposter!
                    You keep sighing
                    to keep us from asking questions

about the owner of this gold.
Otherwise
you're no more than a man
such as my husband
poor and churlish.
I'll not charge you for the bread you've eaten
if you quickly depart.

Miller With what horse?
And where to?
Doors are all closed to me.

Woman Only here
as if in a caravanserai
the door is open.
I told this little man to mend the bolt
but he didn't do it.

Miller The sun and the moon are in opposition.
There's no respite anywhere.
The world lies in wait for me.
Why do you moan?

Girl My chest, my belly.
I have a pain in both.

Miller It's from hunger, dear girl.
This is what I learned today.
In Ctesiphon
I knew nothing about this world.

             Groans never reached my ears.
             I had turned my back to the world.
             And now
             the world has turned its back to me.
             Why do you moan?

Girl   My pain
             my pains!

Miller   Yes, you've already told me.
             Why did I forget, then?
             In Ctesiphon
             I closed the doors
             one by one
             to myself.
             But here
             I found no doors...

             [Pause]

             With gold coins
             I'll buy the mill from you.
             Tell me miller
             how much?

Woman   *[To girl]*
             He wants us to put a price on this ruin.

Miller   *[To woman]*
             You be the miller
             and say what I answered.

	Take the whole sack! Is there no one to sell me this ruin of a mill for pieces of gold?
Woman	*[With a sieve on her head]* There's no profit in this trade, man. We're helpless and bankrupt. The millstone is worn out. The columns are broken. And we've already eaten our draft animal.
Miller	Ah, yes. I've heard that horses have trampled on their riders and obedient dogs bare their teeth to their masters. No matter. Here, there are pieces of gold! Why are you moaning?
Girl	I have a burning heart! Other than the wound it has engraved on in my soul this mill shall yield no profit.
Miller	You should run away!
Woman	He is trying to rid himself of the coins. Nowadays possessing gold means trouble and he who has it

	is not safe. Are there people lying in wait outside. And are we to die for your sake?
Miller	Count!
Woman	Stolen coins!
Girl	He cannot be a thief. Robbers spend their money more wisely.
Woman	What use is this ruin to you? The rafters are falling off and the neighbours have all run away. What do you want it for if not as a mill?
Miller	Suicide.
Commander	Suicide?
Woman	That is what he said.
Miller	Suicide. *[To girl]* Why do you laugh?
Girl	I didn't laugh.
Woman	How much?

Miller All that I have.

Woman You're teasing us for sure.
It's a mean joke
to give hope
and then take it back
and laugh heartily at your dupes.

Girl When will you heartily laugh at us?
What's the use of laughing at us?

Miller It's the world that's laughing at *me*.
Don't moan!
Don't moan!
All the coins!

Woman I accept.

Miller But there's a condition.

Girl What?

Woman I knew it couldn't be without a hitch.
Why,
out with it, damn you!

Miller My hands do not obey me.

Woman Are you afraid?

Miller The dagger does not obey my hand.

Commander Kings are without fear.
They're not without death
but surely without fear.

Girl Are you afraid of death
as you are of life?

Miller With all my being.

Mubad Did he, the King
declare that he was afraid?

Woman With all his bones.

Commander I do not hear!
I will not listen!

Captain In the army of liars
you're the Commander.
Did the King
in his own words
declare that he was afraid?

Woman Say, King
did I hear you right?
Did you say you were afraid?

Miller To my very roots.

Commander Ill stars be cursed!

Miller   Yes
I'll give you all the coins
if you help me.

Woman   What help?

Miller   Strike the dagger!

Commander Do you hear?
He's trying to disown his guilt.

Miller   In a way
that I will not know when or how!
Stay with me a day
then suddenly
from behind
in sleep
whichever way you wish.
Only don't let me know when!

Woman   This is murder, not help!

Miller   My saddlebag is full of coins.
A whole load of them.
Say, say what my answer was then!

Woman   The miller said:
"Woman!
Whore!
Beware!
I begin to understand

what it means to be a king.
And if it is such a frightening business
why is it that lords and heroes
seek it so dearly?
Look how he moans!"

Miller My enemies' thirst for my blood
and I'm weary of living.
Ah
if only my horse had not run away!

Woman To tell you the truth
I, too
wish him dead.
Had he not been what he is
my lot would not have been so grim.
And yet
I am a man
with clean hands.
My bread was of rye
but never soaked in blood.
Let me look for an omen in the dust.
Say something woman!
Is it good or bad?
You girl!
Come and be the miller's wife
and say what my answer was.

Girl *[Laughingly]*
I, the miller's wife?
Ah, miller

	keep me at your side for a while!

Woman Impudent wretch!
Be the miller's wife
and listen to what the King has to say!

Miller I wish I could leave
and be a shepherd.
Everyone can run away
except the king.

Girl Kings always run away
and we're the executioner's prey.

Miller Not always.
You can invoke their gods
hold their stirrup
make way for them
and then you'll be one of them.
The inferior
thus become superior
and you shall continue to pay tribute.
No, there's no blame.
You cannot kill a nation
but you can slay a king.
And once the king is dead
the nation dies.

Woman What sound is this?

Girl It's the coins!

Miller   A whole sack full of them.

Woman   Do you hear?

Girl   Gold was of use to me
when I could save my little boy
when I could buy medicine
for my little daughter.
Today
left alone in the desert
without a soul in sight
what should I do with gold?

Miller   There'll be an end to grief.
People shall return.
Ruins will be reclaimed
and inhabited by people.
Stay and welcome happiness!

Woman   Happiness?
With enemies around?

Miller   Hide your treasure
and no one will know.
This is a time-honoured practice.

Woman   *[To girl]*
Do you hear, woman?
He makes me wonder.
What is to be done?
Our water shall turn into blood

you say?
But listen!
This is the voice of our daughter
burning with fever
and moaning from pain.
And she'll take a husband some day
and she'll need all those coins.
Hey, what say you?
What is to be done?

Girl Why do you ask *me*
when you know the answer?
Why, you're already whetting your knife!
It is clear he's testing our loyalty
measuring our hospitality
and as soon as you comply
he'll reveal his other face.
The smouldering temper
shall burst out into flames
and consume us all.
Therefore
do not comply;
be furious instead
and season your remarks
with many an oath.
He may then be satisfied
and
if he's truly the King
he may give you a few coins.
Otherwise
what mad man would be king

| | and ask for death?
| | Lend no ear to this fable.
| | It is nothing but a trick.

Woman   I thought as much myself.
            Having taken us for dupes
            he's now testing us variously.
            No, guest!
            Be whoever you are
            but know that I am a miller
            not a bandit!

Commander Now that he's not here
              every lie looks like the truth.

Woman   *[Desperate]*
            My husband offered him a bed
            a bite
            and a cup.

Mubad   Is this the bed?

Woman   He gave him what he had.

Mubad   And this, the cup?

Woman   We're not to blame
            if it's cracked.

Mubad   There's hospitality for you, masters!

Woman   He suffered evil
              but did no evil.
              The King asked him thrice
              to kill him for coins
              and thrice he refused.

Mubad   These words are but wind, o host of liars!
              He
              the possessor of all possessors
              the spleeny sovereign
              was not a man to kneel.
              Would a king such as he
              kill himself?
              Your mouths be filled with dust!
              And if it be otherwise
              give me solid proof!

Commander Ay, proof, proof!

Captain   Something prickles my mind.
              Ay
              now that this world is disjointed
              I can
              without fear
              say something
              even though I belong to lower ranks.

Commander What is this?
              Is it about the King
              or his slayers?

Captain   We did not lose him in the storm;
               he fled from us.

Mubad   The sovereign, you say
               fled from his subjects?

Captain   May Ahurâ Mazdâ forgive me a
               thousand times!
               Kingship to him was no longer anything
               but a precipice to fall from.
               He ran away from his stars
               not his subjects.
               I saw him saddling his horse.

Commander Were you not the warrior I know
               I would have taken you for an enemy.

Captain   I saw him put his foot
               furtively
               in the stirrup.

Commander The sovereign
               for whom the stirrup
               had always been held by slaves?
               Now I know why you're still in lower
               ranks!

Captain   I'm an old man, Commander.
               Be angry with me
               but do not shout at me.
               If I'm wrong

	tell me and tell me why!
Commander	Everyone knows that the King was a peerless slayer of lions a match for dragons and great, in the eyes of the warlike deity the supportive Bahrâm. Would an ocean-hearted sovereign on meeting a handful of desert-dwellers attempt to kill himself?
Miller	He commanded me.
Girl	Speak!
Miller	He commanded me.
Woman	*[Holding her ears]* Never, never!
Miller	He commanded me twice thrice four times.
Woman	*[Having pulled a sack on her head]* We've never killed a guest.
Miller	Is there nothing in the Books of Counsel on respecting the will of a king?

Mubad	There is.
It is written that the tidings of Ahurâ
reside in the earthly vessel of a king.

Miller	So, here's the command of Ahurâ Mazdâ!

Woman	I hear nothing.

Miller	He who obeys not the command
shall have an end
darker than shameful death.
Deceitful demons
shall crush his limbs
and for nine thousand years
he shall be prey to nightmares
under the earth.
Now that pure gold does not arouse you
from the lofty pedestal of kingship
high above your shoulder
from the midst of Ahurâi glory
do I command you, o man, miller
to slay me!
Are you not afraid?

Woman	If you're the King
you have people following you.
Those are the ones
I am afraid of.

Miller	Has death, too
turned its back on me?

Woman   O King!
You said that if you die
a nation dies.
How could I dip my hands
in the blood of a nation?

Girl   Kill him, man!
Perhaps a new nation
shall be born out of his death.

Woman   I'm neither a nurse
nor a midwife.
I am a miller.
I give people bread.
This is the only thing I have.

Miller   The world has chosen you
to shed my blood, man!
The Tazian army followed us everywhere:
yelling
roaring
and clamouring.
An army
thick and tangled
with a banner the colour of dark smoke.
Everything has turned away from me
except this army
that follows me
like my own shadow.

Woman   Your enemy, o King

                    is not this army
                    but the people's plight
                    which you yourself
                    have brought about.
                    Otherwise
                    how could a handful of men
                    achieve by themselves
                    anything so momentous?

Mubad   Many fire-temples are still intact.
                 With warm words
                 people should be taught
                 how to war.

Woman   Do not prattle, priest!
                 Having been oppressed for so long
                 people no longer believe in you.

Commander Heavens be cursed!
               In the past
               anyone speaking in that vein
               would have had his tongue pulled out of
               his gullet.

Woman   What other attainments can you boast of
                 besides pulling tongues out of people's
                 gullets?

Captain   I change my verdict.

Commander Ours cannot be changed!

Miller   You, man
               are chosen by providence.
               Once again
               I command you, miller
               to entertain me with my own blood.

Girl   To disobey the King, he says
               is to challenge Ahurâ Mazdâ.

Miller   Ay
               and throughout the kingdom of Persia
               no one has ever disobeyed
               the King of Kings.

Woman   Is that true?
               Then I am pleased.
               Now order the Tazians to retreat!

Miller   You scoff at me.

Woman   Your command was obeyed
               only in Ctesiphon
               and not here.

Miller   Did you hear?
               I disobeyed.

Commander Is it just
               that slaves should disobey
               sovereigns?

Woman I don't understand.
Had he killed him
he would've been a murderer
and now
he is disobedient.
What should he have done, then?

Miller Nothing, woman.
Sin is born with us.
And my twin mate
which is the nearest thing to my soul
is called
destitution.

[Enters Soldier]

Soldier Ladders proved very useful.
I told foot-soldiers
to raise a crypt with stones
instead of digging one.
The earth is hard
and the spade worn out
but corpses cannot be left
without a grave.
Apart from all this
I cannot find a pick.

Commander Has the man confessed to anything?

Soldier He mumbles something
but we do not understand him.

An oil-less wick.
Perhaps the masters
will get something out of him.
Shall I fetch him?

Mubad No!
It's unbelievable
that the miller was not seduced by gold;
unbelievable
that he did not strike the dagger;
unbelievable
that he did not slay the King.
You must indeed have killed him
and other than this
everything is unbelievable.

Soldier The gibbet is set.
It only needs a piece of rope.

Woman There's rope in the cellar.
You've ruined me.
Don't take more than you need.
Where did you take the wood from?
Leave the leftovers!

Soldier *[Going out]*
If you want him alive
beat the drum
but if you want his head
blow the horn!

Woman   To those whose hands are tied
              you're a champion
              you block-head, you ape!

Commander Silence!
              Who told you to speak?

Woman   This is my house
              and I speak as I please.
              I shall not sell my husband
              cheaply to death.

Mubad   Stay!
              Do not flounce, you dismal heretic!
              Our verdict will not change.
              Did you not hear
              that the gibbet was set?

Woman   Why should I not do what I can?
              May your frame
              never enjoy freedom again, Commander
              for you brought untimely death to our
              house!

Captain   Even now
              that edicts of this vast land are changing
              the rich are
              as always
              delivered
              and the weak are kept in bonds.
              Why did you not run away?

Miller   I had no mule
to pack my wares on.

Girl   The world is lying in wait
for my chastity.
All things have conspired
to add to my misery.
The mule dies
the neighbour goes away
the millstone breaks
and someone brings his death here.

Woman   When he lost all hope of death
the stranger devised a new stratagem.

Miller   He tried to rouse my anger.

Girl   *[Weeping]*
Why was not your anger roused?

Miller   He looked and looked and looked
at my face.

Woman   Fie!

Miller   Then spat at it.

Girl   Stop, stop, stop!

Miller   He hit me in the chest.

Girl   O, stone-hearted creature
bandit
evil-eyed!

Woman   *[With mask]*
O, you idiot!
For so many long years
you've turned a mill
in the midst of this desert
eating rye bread and dry dates.
Is there no power of vengeance in you?
Am I not your King
as well as your enemy?
You haven't seen my palace in Ctesiphon.
We don't sleep on straw there.
You haven't seen our Negârestân Carpet
with warps of gold and woofs of silver
patterned with trees and birds and
flowers
all inlaid with priceless gems.
I have a chess set
with rows of red and yellow rubies.
And a set of backgammon
made of clear emeralds.
I have thirty two thousand pieces of
precious rubies.
Do you know?
And the Treasure of the Bride
and the Green Treasure
and the Treasure of the Wind
and the Treasure of the Regal Brocade

and the Burnt Treasure
and the Arched Throne
and the Great Tent
and the Golden Palace
and twelve thousand slave-girls.
Should more be said?
Are you not roused to anger?
Is there no power of vengeance in you?

Miller I told him:
"O man," I said, "whoever you are
whether a King
a beggar in rags
or a highway man
do not rouse my anger!
My heart swells
and I might do harm
either to you
or to myself."

Woman Twelve hundred elephants
thirteen thousand camels of burden
and the Game Garden
and the Garden of the Beheaded Hero
and the Emerald Garden
and the Garden of the Twelve Thousand
Greyhounds
and seven hundred thousand horsemen
and three hundred thousand foot-soldiers
and one hundred thousand riding horses

                    and one hundred thousand gold
scabbards;
and every year
I receive
seven hundred and ninety-five times a
million drachmas
from every direction.

Miller   I told him:
"You evil-wisher
loose-tongued babbler
you oppressor!
Do not rouse my anger!
I'm a man of ripe age
and soon I shall be gone.
Misfortune has made me cruel.
And I do not wish to harm my guest."

Woman   He was laughing.
He reached for the whip
and took him to task:
"O man," he said,
"in you, there's not the courage of an
experienced slave.
To you
foulness is clean
and disgrace counts as virtue.
You do not value your King as a king.
I had guard dogs
whose voice I haven't heard for some time.
Fall on your feet as dogs do!

Like my dogs
walk on all fours
and bark!
My nimble horse has not given me a
ride for two days.
Where's the saddle?
I would put it on you.
O, man
tell your wife to come to my bed
quick, quick!"

Miller *[Falling on woman's feet]*
O, King
do not beat me
do not make me the laughing stock of
people!
I'm a man with little patience left
and I might raise my hand against you.
Let me be!
Leave me!

Woman Your tongue be cut
and your lips, sutured!
You prattle so
and you babble.
You foolish
dastardly villain
step aside
and do not block my way!
In this darkness
I've just begun to notice your daughter

                who
                despite her ailments
                is not at all bad
                and her lips are the colour of jujube.
                And she's beginning to get ripe.
                Invite me to the fruits of her flesh!

Miller   O, King
                you say things that I do not understand.

Woman   If you do not understand *my* language
                you *will* that of the whip!

Miller   I know you want to test me.
                You fathom my fidelity.
                There's no question about my fidelity
                none.
                Do not make me more despicable than I
                am.
                O, King
                let me kiss your knees!

Girl   O, King
                he has fallen on his knees.
                Isn't that enough?

Woman   Did you say: "on his knees"?
                He has yet to rub his head in the dust.
                Go, down in the dust
                and lie there
                until I give your daughter

	the honor of lying under me!
Girl	What do you want from me?
Woman	Jujubes and almonds laced with sugar!
Girl	No! *[Runs away]* Save me father! Save me!
Miller	*[Holds his ears]* No, no, no this is all a trial for me. All this is just to test me.
Woman	You're ripe and ready, girl! Do you prefer the sweet tongue or the serpent whip?
Miller	*[Holding his eyes]* I shall not be angry no I shall not be angry!
Girl	Deliver me, father! The dagger is on my throat. Deliver me!

Commander A more shameful story
has never been forged.
How could our sovereign crave
a base slave-girl?
He who had three thousand women in
Ctesiphon
each one better than the other.

Girl *[Appears from behind the millstone]*
Would that there was a sack of flour here
and I could pour it on my head
and turn white all over!

Miller My daughter
she was never so lost and helpless
with a dead look in her eyes.

Girl You're tall
and twice as wide as I am.
Your might challenges my chastity.
And through the casement
I watch the devil
riding away on a grey horse.

Miller No, no!
He wanted to fathom my fidelity.
To raise a hand against the King:
such an infernal sin!
No, not me!
And now a hell
more fearsome

burns me from within.
What is this boiling river
running through my veins?
And this turmoil
lodged in my heart?
I shall slay him.
Ay, there's a millstone in my heart.

[Falls on the corpse and stabs it]

Girl   *[Glad and proud]*
I pity the slain man.
I pity the slain man.

Woman   *[Without mask]*
Cut be your tongue!

[To man]
Strike the dagger harder!

Miller   *[Still stabbing]*
I shall slay him twice
thrice
four times...

Woman   Strike, strike!

Miller   *[Stops, out of breath]*
I slew him.
Ay, and I am glad.

Commander You saw everything with your own eyes.
And the words blurted out by this beast
are they not enough
to prove his guilt
to the world?

Mubad The truth finally spoke up.
Ay, an honest account
cried itself out
and we all heard it.

Commander This is our justice!

Woman But you did *not* kill him!

Miller No, I did not!

Mubad What useless concealment!

Miller I did not kill him.
That was a false account.

Mubad Wherefore lie?

Miller I feared that you would take me
for a shameless father.
I did not kill him
until he began to play with me.

Commander Play?

Mubad What play?

Woman *[With mask]*
Well did I call myself king
and fooled you
to get food
bed
and bedmate.
Hah, well did I make sport of you.
Well did I trick you with games.
Who am I
even to be made a door-keeper?
Any vagabond can walk in
and call himself a king
and slip into your daughter's bed.
Hah?
How easily, how easily!

Miller Not so easily
not so.
Where's my club?

Woman Her flesh was good.
Happy hospitality!

Miller Where's my club?
Give me my stick!
Hold my hand up!
Pull out the rafter, ho!

Mubad Do you hear?

>   You did hear in this court
>   that he cried out for his club.

Commander To kill the King!

Woman Who said I was the King?
Does my countenance shine with divine
light?
Do I have an army
or a palace
or comely slave-girls?
Do I have a nation?

Girl He has a treasure with him.

Woman I've stolen it.

Girl From whom
ask him!

Woman From you.
Add up the wages of all your days
would they not add up to a treasure?

Miller The days of my life.
Ah, I've forgotten when they began.

Woman I stole all your days.

Miller Then you *are* the King!
How could it be otherwise?

The days of my life.
Always I wished
to plead justice with the King
and now
that he's here
with whom should I plead justice?
Give back what you took from me, o King!
The days of my life
my wasted hopes
and my daughter's chastity!

Girl   *[Shrieks]*
Blood!
Blood!

Woman   *[Takes off the mask]*
Blood gushed out of his mouth.

Girl   That's not enough!

Woman   *[Sits above the head of the corpse]*
Tell me, King
how did you find my daughter?
Did she give you a good ride?

Girl   *[Weeping]*
It rained all night
and he stood alone before me.

Woman   Speak, o mighty King!
Was she easy-paced

	when giving the ride?
Miller	*[Roaring, falls on the corpse and stabs it]* I... killed... him!
Woman	Did you enjoy her? Was she tame when you lay upon her and rode within her?
Miller	My club!
Woman	Strike!
Miller	Days of my life!
Woman	Strike!
Miller	All my wages!
Woman	Strike!
Girl	Strike!
Miller	I slew him.
Girl	I pity the slain man I pity the slain man. *[Sits down]*

	Ah, father why did they kill you?
Woman	Be silent and stop your follies!
Girl	Ah, father, father! What did they do to you?
Woman	Not another word.
Girl	Ah, father! Why did they kill you?
Captain	How? Do you hear? What does she say?
Girl	He who sleeps here is my father. A poor miller who received no reward from life not even after his death.
Commander	What are you saying? Is this not the blood-covered countenance of the King?
Woman	You should know that she has lost her wits.
Girl	*[Falls on the corpse]*

Father
speak and answer them!

[She gets up]

My child, my child
why did I abandon you?

Mubad   Do you hear?
The dead man speaks.
Nothing like this has ever been written
in the sacred books.
Truth is calling us
from the other world.

Commander May my memory be obliterated!
Hold them and let me see.
And you
get all of you together!
This is our war council.
Quick!
It is said that this is not the body of the
King.
Has anyone seen his face at close range?

Captain   No one ever dared to look at his
majestic countenance;
and he did not show his face to everyone.

Commander Were you not the first
to recognize the King

	on seeing his lacerated corpse?
Captain	I recognized him by his crown
for I had never seen him
without his dazzling mask of pure gold.
Commander	O, Head of all Priests
Guardian of the Luminous Fire-Temple
speak!
You had seen him many times.
Mubad	I had, indeed
but not with his face blue
with the colour of death
and speckled with dried blood
his mouth half open
his eyes fixed upon the rafters
and his whole countenance
bearing signs of deadly pain.
Commander	I myself had never encountered him
except when he wore his gilded helmet
or sat behind a screen.
It is, therefore, difficult for me
to say how far that glory is
from this blood-covered corpse.
Captain	What should be done now?
In this sorry state
even the King's bedmates
could not recognize him

| | let alone the servants
            who kept their heads bowed
            all the time.

Commander If he is the miller
            then where's the King?

Woman   I told you thrice
            that he fled in disguise
            for the only thing he had in mind
            was to get away.
            I've nothing more to say
            even though your disbelief
            may lead to my ruin.

Mubad   *[Beats the corpse]*
            Woe betide us
            if this dead man
            should only be
            a nameless miller!
            For I graced him
            with the Kings' Prayer.

Woman   Fie!
            What days are these?
            Even now that the whole kingdom
            is being overrun by the enemy
            our brave and warlike commanders
            continue to wreak vengeance
            on humble folk.

Captain Silence!

[Soldier enters]

Soldier Where's the mortar?

Girl Stand straight, Soldier!
What do you want the mortar for?

Soldier The miller's bones are to be pounded.

Woman There's the mortar
and here's the oven.
Anything else that you want?

Soldier Only an axe!

Woman Read out the scroll of victory
and sound the trumpet
for you've vanquished
the humble
and the empty-handed!

Commander If that's the miller's corpse
who *this* man is?

Soldier *[Laughing]*
The enemy prisoner is ready to die
but he won't speak.
Yet he keeps mumbling something.

Captain   It should be found out
whether the Tazians are coming
or going.

Mubad   That indeed is necessary!

Commander *[To miller]*
Who are you, man?

Woman   Can we speak together
in private
for a few moments?
We three?
A family council.

Commander Why not
if thinking together
can add to your wisdom.

Mubad   Why not, indeed
if it brings perspicacity
to those who indulge their folly.

Commander And if it brings about
what we're after
ponder together
and ponder more.
But woe betide you
if it doesn't yield the knowledge we seek!

[To Soldier]

Wait outside
but watch the doors.
These are your prisoners.

[To Captain]
Let all exits be blocked!

[To Mubad]
Off we go!

[To woman]
And when we return
that man's face
must be cleared of flour
and all that covers it.

[To Captain]
Show me where the Tazian captive is.

[Exeunt]

Soldier What is it
that you should say
and we must not hear?

Woman Get lost!

Soldier I wish one of you would run away!
- My lance will be lying in wait.
You would make good meat
for my skewer!

                    Pity my lance is poisoned.
                    To hell!

                    [Exit]

Miller   *[Agitated]*
                    What's on your mind, woman?

Woman   Fool, there's no escape!
                    If they take this carcass
                    to be the corpse of the fallen King
                    they'll spill our blood.
                    We must say and repeat
                    that this is not the King.

Girl   We all know
                    that this corpse
                    is that of the miller.

Miller   If this is the miller
                    then who am I?

Woman   This is the question
                    soon to be asked.

Miller   If I'm not the miller
                    then I must be the King
                    right?

Woman   No other way.
                    If you be not the King

| | then you'll be the King's killer;
| | and we shall all die a painful death.
| | Which is better:
| | to be the King
| | or die?

Miller   Hum!
             You have a point there!

Girl   *[Weeping]*
             You never liked my father.
             You were never kind to him
             or shared your bed with him.
             O you
             you never gave yourself to him
             and he has always
             mourned his own distress and poverty
             and your unkindliness.
             I shall never be reconciled to you.

Woman   What could I have done
             except to turn
             all the days of my life
             into night
             beside him
             in this dungeon?
             And to be a beast of burden
             such as himself?
             Like two mules
             together
             turning the millstone.

| | Don't make me even more regretful
for having born you.
I never expected gratitude from you
for having brought you to this world. |
|---------|---|
| **Miller** | Enough!
Stop it, girl! |
| **Girl** | Don't speak with me!
Don't touch me, you stranger! |
| **Miller** | It is *me*, fool!
Don't you know me? |
| **Girl** | I know you well.
I know what manner of man you are.
Had there been buyers for me
doubtless you would have sold me
for one smile from this woman. |
| **Woman** | What can I do, my beloved?
Your sellers are my buyers. |
| **Miller** | Cut the quarrel short!
While here we scuffle
they raise our graves outside
stone upon stone
and make my gibbet steady.
So, be silent! |
| **Girl** | Why should I not weep |

| | since my poor father perished
            before my very eyes?

Woman | O mother's darling
            do not make my heart bleed!

Miller | Why does she think me dead?
            Have I ever lived in your eyes?
            Ah, what am I saying?
            I was born in this crypt.
            I was already a dead man
            stepping into a cold grave.
            And now
            before seeing the light of the world
            I'm passing
            from one death to another.

Girl | *[Falls on the corpse]*
            Father, father
            why did you not take me with you?

Miller | She truly believes him
            to be the miller!

Woman | It seems so.
            And that's not a bad thing.
            Her madness leads to profit
            while wisdom
            yields nothing but loss.
            Ah, my daughter!
            Misfortune has crushed her so

and she no longer knows who she is.
God knows
how long she'll thus continue
and do as she does.

[Commander and others enter]

Commander Did you hear their words?

Soldier No, Commander
I only peeped through the hole in the door.

Commander Before he died
that wretched little captive
as a result of what he said
made us think of gathering an army
as quickly as we could.
The Tazians have pushed directly eastwards
so they're getting further away from here.

Soldier Further away?

Commander Yes
and this stands to reason
and tallies with the forecasts of war experts.

Soldier Getting further away!
What glad tidings!

>   So fortune smiles on us.

Commander   Indeed
                   it would've been great news
                   if the King were still alive.

                   [To woman]
                   Did the meeting of your minds
                   bear any fruit?

Woman   We only watered the tree.

Commander   A ripe fruit, hah
                   which should be picked.
                   Be quicker!

Woman   It's not easy.
                   O priest
                   I must break an oath.
                   Is this admissible?

Mubad   There's only one way
                   and that's the path of truth.
                   Everything else is a byway.

Woman   The girl was right.
                   The miller sleeps here.

Commander   What did you say?

Mubad   Consolidate everything you say

	with a deadly oath!
Woman	I swear by the lives of all priests!
Mubad	So, this dead man is the miller.
	[He kicks the corpse]
	And who is *this* man?
Woman	*[Putting clothes on him]* The King!
Commander	Did you hear?
Captain	Unbelievable!
Woman	Yes, noble knights and commanders. The miller died his own death. And this living standing man, here is the King who wanted to be lost to himself. So, he thus garbed his frame.
Commander	Is this not a dream come true?
Mubad	Why did you not say this at first?
Woman	I had sworn to hide his secret.

Commander And he was testing us
all of us;
do you hear?
I hope I haven't used any strong words.
I am indeed fortunate
to have passed this test with honor.

Captain *[Kneels]*
O, King!

Woman Look at your sword of justice
becoming blunt now!
The death of the miller
shall pass without punishment.
O yes
look at your justice!

Commander What is the King's command?

Miller Get out of my way!
Leave me to my solitude
and never say you've seen me!

Captain Has the King no more wishes?

Woman He won't accept his own kingship.

Miller I didn't want to be surrounded by brave knights
and to be talked about everywhere.
I meant to get away

                and cast no shadow.
                So I thought it best
                to be taken for dead.
                And I put on these clothes.

Mubad   These are wise words.

Commander Great is the King's suffering.
                Our backs be bent before you, o King!

Captain   If you're the King
                pronounce my name!

Woman   Why should the King know
                the names of his servants?

Captain   That's a kingly answer!
                But there should be a witness.
                Is there no one
                among the military
                who's seen the King?

Commander Are you testing the King?

Captain   Ay
                now that his face
                is cleared of dust
                perhaps some can distinguish in him
                truth from falsehood.

Soldier   *[Falls on the ground]*

If you spare me
I shall confess my unforgivable sin.
Ay
Once, stealthily, I looked
at the shining face of the King
but from far away.
He was in hunting grounds
and there was the hubbub of the falconers
when my eyes caught his sight
- only for a short moment.
And I don't truly know
if that was the true face of the King
or he had put on a false face.
He had a bow in one hand
and a cup in the other.
But these are useless signs
for I've heard
that in order not to be recognized
the King has placed his hair and beard
in the hands of his hairdresser.
How then could he be recognized?

Mubad Indeed he couldn't.

[Comes forward]
The King smelt sweet
with the scent of cardamoms
and rose-water.
And here
there's only the smell of must
and dampness.

But I know a way.
O man
put on the King's crown
and wear his robe!

Woman Here!

Soldier No, this is not him.
With this crown and robe
I swear
he's far more magnificent than our
King!

Commander Another test!

Mubad Walk
laugh
turn around
close your eyes
gloat
shout
cry out
whisper
open your arms
put your hands to your sides
cross your hands
[wearily]
cannot be told.

Captain But these are not the hands of a King.
Hands so rough and worked

	callous and crusty.
Miller	*[Claps his hands]* Are they not?
Mubad	By heavens they are. The war-battered hands of a warlike, club-wielding King that have pulled many a bow string thrown many a javelin shot many an arrow wielded many a sword and ripped many a chain mail. Ah, I don't recall the name of the best of the King's horses.
Woman	Shabrang!
Mubad	And the best bird?
Woman	Shabâviz!
Mubad	And the best woman?
Woman	Shabâhang!
Commander	If you're the King then tell us the number of chambers in Ctesiphon palace!

Woman The Dark Chamber for rebels
the Ruby Chamber for women
and the Chrysolite Chamber for
musicians.
Any other question?

Commander He knows.
He knows.
Give us another sign!

Woman The Negârestân Carpet
with one thousand one hundred and
eleven jewels.

Commander He knows;
do you hear?

Mubad The exact number of the King's wives
is my exclusive knowledge.
If you're the King
tell it!

Woman Two hundred and ten.

Mubad Astonishing!
These are all correct.

Miller *[To woman]*
How do you know all this?

Woman You told me;

	don't you remember, King?
Miller	I did not.
Woman	You told me the number of corridors jewels and bed chambers. Who else could have told me?
Miller	He! When he drove me into the rain. *He* told you the King!
Woman	You're the King!
Miller	No he's not me. I am I myself the miller. I am a man without wealth or fortune and I have my hands in blood up to my elbow. Say *he* told you all this!
Woman	Indeed, he did.
Girl	Indeed, he did.

Commander Separate them!
What is the matter?

Girl The matter?

[Begins to walk]

I saw it with my own eyes

[smiling]

I
whom they took, for nobody.

Miller Speak!

Girl He wanted to seduce my mother.

Woman That's not true.

Girl *[To miller]*
Your wife!

Commander Do not slander our King!

Girl He waylaid you, miller.

Commander Our King?

Girl Pouring venom!

Miller   I don't mind this woman
                for she's been held in many arms
                before.

Woman   Coward!

Miller   I'm no fool.

Woman   We all have our clients.

Miller   Neighbours?

Woman   Had I not tried
                who would've given us bread?

Girl   What harm have you not done to my
                father!

Woman   Did I harm you
                by saving you from starvation
                when we had nothing?

Mubad   Ah, what are they saying?
                With all this evil talk
                Ahurâ Mazdâ cannot be here.
                It is time for the moon
                to change colour
                and the sun
                to show fearsome signs.
                There has grown conflict
                between my knowledge

and my faith
and between wisdom
and love.
It looks like the end of Ahurâi millennium.
We must send
books of Counsel
to the four corners
of the land of Iran.

Woman Send Books of Counsel
by all means, Mubad
but let them be accompanied
by some bread.
We people
have a surfeit of counsel
and crave for bread.

Captain I'm not a man of knowledge, Mubad;
you who are
say something.

Woman Yes, protest!
Who could blame me?
For long years
I've been waiting for deliverance.

Girl *[Begins to walk]*
He wanted to seduce my mother.
He whispered in darkness
and there was only the tongue of fire
between them.

Miller   Where was I?

Girl   Out in the rain!

Miller   Was it not early evening?

Girl   When the storm swirled
and spiraled
and began to roar
and at last
ended in blizzard and hailstone.
Yes
even then
the King was still trying
to belittle the miller...
Forcing him to bark
like a dog!

[Miller falls down and barks]

Girl   Louder!
Louder!
Give me that gilded crown
and that girdle!
And now tell me, once again
who I am!

Miller   My Liege
you're the King.

Girl   And you, beggar's son

	who are *you*?
Miller	Your humble dog, the miller.
Girl	And what you have... whom does it come from you wretched, evil-eyed creature?
Miller	All we have comes from the King.
Woman	What are you saying, man? We don't have *anything*!
Miller	Even that comes from the King.
Girl	The girl was my kingly portion. Did you know that? Oh!
Miller	What happened?
Girl	Arrows of misfortune rain from the sky. I'm the target of them all. Their legions are endless. With dishevelled hair and bedraggled, belted frames they sit astride black saddles with banners uplifted.
Miller	Were they so near?

Girl	The enemy? May be they are far away now. It seems clear that the world does not wish me dead. So, I'll have to stay alive!
Woman	Even rats are running away. It is cold. What a rain! Out of the blizzard I seem to hear a thousand dirges.
Girl	Perhaps they shall return. Fetch some fire! Where's the firewood? I looked at the sky. It is raining fast. Like an inverted sea. What's this?
Miller	A sword.
Girl	For your breast! You did not kill me, miller you were more frightened than I had thought. You did not even have the guts to bring down the stick you had raised.
Miller	I'm a harmless man.

Woman [*Shrieks*]
It is cold.

Miller What makes you shriek?

Woman You!
You, man!
You, kind-hearted man
who broke your stick on your knee
when you should've cracked his skull.
Must we sit now
and watch the ruffians come
and sweep away your household
and disgrace you?

Miller I am a hospitable man.

Woman You didn't kill the man
who held the key
to our fortune.

Miller Don't look at me so
with bleeding eyes!

Woman Was it not you
who fell on his feet
like a dog?

Girl What is this secret parley?

Woman He's a harmless man.

Girl   Huh!
That is well, my good man.
You know that
one is rewarded with gold
and punished with sword.
I'm cold to my bones.
Fetch some firewood.
Fire
and something to eat.
A sheep.

Miller   Which sheep?
There's famine among people.
Many have starved to death.

Girl   Ah, if only my horse had not run away…

Miller   We would've eaten it together!

Girl   Are you making yourself equal to a king?

Miller   You've already made yourself equal to a beggar.

Girl   Go to the village.
Peddlers or hucksters
or anyone
who might have a sheep
must know
that it belongs to the King.
Use force

	Steal!
	You all belong to the race of robbers.
Miller	It is cold.
	Do not send me away in this blizzard!
Girl	Take a lamp...
	And do not come back
	without some well-prepared victual!
Miller	The village is far away
	four miles, perhaps.
Girl	Better if you find a roast!
	Did you hear?
	Bring me a roast for dinner
	or a sheep!
Miller	It is late.
	I'll get lost.
	It's dark and windy
	and there's lashing rain.
Girl	What about the King's command?
Miller	Humbly I go
	this minute.
Girl	Why
	no beast would venture into the desert
	in this black rainy night.

| | I've become suspicious of you, man.
My heart has turned against you.
You're not foolishly contemplating
to go and reveal the King's secret, are you? |

Miller I had no such an intention.

Girl You know my whereabouts.
And there are those
who'd give you gold
for a sign of me.

Miller *You* put this thought into my head, King!

Girl Then, I shall keep your wife and daughter
as hostages here
and I hold a naked sword
in my hand.
When *that* idea crosses your mind
remember this!

Woman No bandit has ever treated us so.

Girl Do you put kings
on the same footing as bandits?

Woman Unlike kings
bandits show mercy to the poor.

Miller I should go.
Is it not time for me

to be delivered from this woman?

Woman From me?
Wherever in the world you may be
having lost your heart
you shall return to me.
Have we not been through this
many times before?

Miller I went.
Under a dark and fearsome rain
in which
the desert could not be told from the
night.
And the universe seemed
like a turbulent sea
a whore of a sea
with its whirlpools.
There
my mill appeared as an inverted ship.
I went.
Far away.
Looking for a few pieces of firewood
and a sheep for food.
But my thoughts were all here
wondering what the King was up to.

Girl Why must I die?
Why should I entrust myself
to the frozen land of death?
The Tazians have lost track of me

in the storm
and I have shaved my chin and head
and gone into disguise
hoping that I shall not be recognized.
One can run away
and live contentedly
for years and years.
It would've been better
if they thought me dead
and stopped looking for me.
I wish I could find a lifeless body
and clothe it with my clothes.
Ah, all is well
except for this woman and her daughter
who've been through the whole story
and can tell it to others.
The girl is witless
and that leaves the woman.

Woman He was with me.
The King and I
alone.
The miller's wife
who has always had to put up
with the scowls of hard-headed
hard-hearted ruffians.
The King is looking at me
from beyond this fire.
What's on his mind?

Girl Hum, this an idea.

	Could she be trapped?
Woman	Fear has conquered me. Is my heart a dove?
Girl	The miller's wife has a fine body. She has suffered and starved. I shall make her look up to me. I shall seduce her.
Woman	What do you want, King?
Girl	Could she be tamed with a bait? Woman! How is your husband?
Woman	He loves me.
Girl	And you?
Woman	I? Do I reveal anything? Have I said anything to make you ask so direct a question? I pity him. Ah, he should not have gone. What am I doing? Ah, what's happening to him?
Girl	Why do you tremble? O woman, why do you moan?

Woman He's suffered much
and I too.
I *too*!

Girl O woman
you've made me desperate.

Woman No.

Girl Come nearer woman!
You make my heart flutter.

Woman You frighten me.

Miller Death to you, woman!

Woman Why?
What pleasure did I ever have with you?
I was young when I stepped into this darkness
my companion
a stone
placed beside another stone.

Girl *[Weeping]*
O father, father
why did they kill you?

Mubad No, dear girl
you were telling the King's story.

Girl	Mother, forgive me. I despise you. *[Shrieks]* I despise you. *[Woman slaps her in the face. Girl's face opens with a smile]* Ah, that was a beautiful slap you gave to the King when he first opened his heart to you.
Woman	Stop, stop! Don't torment me, my girl. You love me. Don't!
Girl	*[Seductively]* This miller is nothing. If you despise him a little if you look for a little happiness be with me!
Woman	Yes he said that and my heart fluttered. Say more, o King!
Girl	I've taken a liking to you, miller's wife. Your body is firm.

| | It's the warmest thing
that could be found in this rainstorm.
I have taken to you! |
|---|---|
| **Woman** | *[Groans]*
Is that true?
Would anyone take my hand? |
Girl	You shall be delivered.
Woman	From the whirlpool!
Girl	And I shall press you in my arms.
Woman	You pressed my daughter in your arms.
Girl	That wasn't for love.
It was all out of weariness.
You know well
that this girl
is not worthy of me.
All that
was nothing but a bluff.
I sought your loathing
yours and the miller's
and I wanted you to kill me
with your own hands
- you and the miller.
Woman	May my hand be cut!

Girl	The likes of me die and the basest animals live.
Woman	You shall not die!
Girl	What did you say?
Woman	How can I be delivered from my husband?
Girl	And I'm looking for a corpse a carcass in King's clothes. How can I find this?
Woman	This is a fearsome thought.
Girl	Everyone will take it to be the King's body. What end more glorious than that for your husband?
Woman	No one is guiltless.
Girl	You and I will sit on one saddle and my treasure shall suffice us forever.
Woman	Shall I be delivered?
Girl	Well, what do you say?
Woman	You're younger.

Girl	And more comely. I used to sit on Tâqdis, the Arched Throne and walk on the Negârestân Carpet with one thousand one hundred and eleven jewels while my two hundred and ten wives followed me.
Woman	In the Ctesiphon Palace?
Girl	Thirty-three corridors in our palace all led to my terrace surrounded by seven chambers: The Dark Chamber for rebels The Ruby Chamber for women The Chrysolite Chamber for musicians... And other chambers.
Woman	Ah, you idiot! So you were listening to all that!
Girl	And more. I'm from earth and water and you from air and fire. For me there's no escape from you no escape!
Woman	Don't torment me!
Girl	Your eyes are burning forests

and the storm is raging in your limbs.
Moan quietly, woman
quiet!

Woman Ah, ah, so you heard everything!

Girl O miller's wife
the miller is nothing.
You close your eyes
and we shall kill him
and wrap him in my regal garments
and run away.
Everyone will think
that the dead man is me.

Woman The girl.
What about the girl?

Girl That foolish slave-girl?
She has no wits!
If she stays alive
the enemy's army
shall pass over her body.

Woman Kill her!

Girl This is a better fate for her.

Woman *[Roaring]*
Kill her!

Girl [Shrieking, withdraws]
My father comes.

[Miller approaches, wild-eyed and stick-in-hand]

From the heart of darkness and storm
he comes
puzzled.

Woman Kill him!

Miller O shameless creature!

[Attacks]
Die!

[Strikes the body. Woman shrieks and throws herself into the arms of the girl]

Yes, he attacked me.
Your King.
With drawn sword.
Like a wild beast.

[Begins to walk]
He was a bold warrior
and his Kâboli sword was peerless.
Like death
he descended upon me
and I killed him.

[He strikes]

Captain Was that not suicide?

Woman *[Yells]*
Where is salvation?

[Soldier enters]

Soldier The gallows is ready.
The grave is dug.
The mortar is beside the gallows
and the oven is blazing.

Miller O woman
and o my daughter
come nearer!
You victims of my poverty!
Now I part with my twin mate misery.
From what I've heard
the advancing enemies
the Tazians
are more like me
than these commanders.
And if I had bread and dates
I'd give it to them.

Commander Break the gallows!
And put out the oven!
My verdict changes.

Mubad Mine too.

Captain And also mine.

Commander The legend stays as it is.
Put this dead body on the gallows!

Soldier The King?

Commander Without delay!
This is the miller.

[To Captain]
Let me know
when this evil deed is done.

[To Mubad]
O priest
should you not sing a hymn?

Captain Let us go.
History is written by the victors.

[With soldier, he picks up the body and goes out]

Commander What're you gazing at?
I shall throw away this Commander's uniform.
This is a hopeless war.
From him

we have inherited a world
we cannot defend.
Hah!
What are you gazing at?

Woman O man, look!
Through the same threshold
where you witnessed the entrance of the
King in rags
look!
In his footsteps
I behold the Tazian army.

[Captain runs in, agitated, with drawn sword]

Captain We were all prey to death
without knowing.
Judgement is not passed yet.
Look at the principle judges
who're just arriving.
A sea of an army!
They neither greet
nor take leave
neither ask questions
nor listen to answers.
They speak the language of the sword.

[Mubad, sword in hand, runs in]

Mubad We're trapped.

The Tazians, Tazians!

[Soldier, with drawn sword, runs in]

Soldier Draw your swords!
Raise your spears!
Javelins!
Drums!

Commander Useless words!
Pray to death
who is standing at the door!
Numberless like sands of the desert
flying around in storm
and blinding the eyes of the world!

Woman Ay
the principle judges are coming now.
With your white banners
you have passed your judgement.
Let us now await
the verdict of the Black Banners.

[Lights go out]

THE PLAYERS' SONG

May those who read this legend
be delivered from the world's thousand treacheries!
May they walk tall
on the proving ground of this world!
On stretching a loving hand
may they not encounter a dagger!
May they not see the day
when they cannot know
friend from foe!
Let us ask forgiveness
for the speaker
and the listener
for the compiler
and the author
who spent much life on this!
Say "Be it so
and be it more so!"

The End.

Death of Yazdgerd was first staged from September 23 to November 11, 1979 at the *Chahar-su* Hall of the *Theatre-e-Shahr* of Tehran with the following cast:

Sussan Taslimi	Woman
Mehdi Hashemi	Miller
Yasaman Arami	Girl
Amin Tarokh	Commander
Mahmoud Behruzian	Mubad
Karim Akbari	Captain
Ya'gub Shakouri	Soldier
Costume Designer	Bahram Beyzaie
Art Director	Iraj Raminfar
Make-up	Farhang Moayyeri
Photography	Aziz Sa'ati
Director	Bahram Beyzaie

Two years after the theatrical production of the play, a cinematic version of Death of Yazdgerd was produced by the same Writer/Director, Bahram Beyzaie, in an old mill in Aran, a small town near the historic city of Kashan.

www.ingramcontent.com/pod-product-compliance
Lightning Source LLC
Chambersburg PA
CBHW020538080526
44583CB00013B/900